15 Essential Habits for Success and Influence

Mastering Personal Development

Rachel R. Page

Copyright message

Table of contents

Table of contents.. 2
Habit 1...9
Habit 2...14
Habit 3...20
Habit 4...25
Habit 5...29
Habit 6...33
Habit 7...37
Habit 8...41
Habit 9...45
Habit 10..49
Habit 11..52
Habit 12..55
Habit 13..58
Habit 14..61
Habit 15..65
Conclusion.. 68

Why this book

15 Essential Habits for Success and Influence: Mastering Personal Development' is your guide to unlocking your full potential. Discover the proven habits that can propel you from mediocrity to greatness, from self-doubt to unshakable confidence. This book provides a blueprint for success, covering goal setting, time management, communication skills, emotional intelligence, and more. It's a transformative journey towards achieving your dreams and leaving a lasting impact on the world. Don't miss the opportunity to master the essential habits that can shape your future.

INTRODUCTION

In the quiet town of Oakville, nestled beneath a canopy of ancient oaks, there lived a man named Samuel. To most, Samuel was an unassuming figure, an unremarkable presence in a world brimming with life's endless possibilities. But what few knew was that Samuel held a secret—a secret that would change the course of his life and inspire those around him in unimaginable ways.

One sunny morning, as the golden light filtered through the leaves, Samuel sat on his porch, lost in thought. He had always dreamt of achieving great things, of making a difference in the world. Yet, life had a way of piling responsibilities and distractions upon him. Day by day, his dreams seemed to drift further and further away.

But that morning, as Samuel sipped his coffee and watched the sun rise, he made a decision that would set the wheels of transformation into motion. He decided to change his life by adopting a set of fifteen essential habits that, when practiced with dedication and purpose, would lead him down a path of success and influence.

Little did Samuel know that this decision would mark the beginning of a remarkable journey—a journey that would take him from mediocrity to greatness, from self-doubt to unshakable confidence, and from obscurity to the forefront of his field.

As we embark on this journey together, you'll discover the very same habits that propelled Samuel to unprecedented heights. You'll learn the art of setting clear goals, harnessing time wisely, mastering communication, and cultivating self-discipline and resilience. You'll explore the power of continuous learning, emotional intelligence, and adaptability. We'll delve into the secrets of networking, problem-solving, and fostering creativity. You'll see how health, wealth, and the art of giving back play vital roles in achieving your aspirations. You'll understand how leadership and influence are within your grasp, and how a lifetime of personal development is both fulfilling and rewarding.

This book is a roadmap to your own transformation, inspired by the story of Samuel and his unwavering commitment to change. These pages hold the keys to unlocking your potential and creating a life filled with success and influence. The journey won't always be easy, but it will be worth it. So, dear reader, prepare to embark on a path that could transform your life, just as it did for Samuel—a journey towards mastering personal development and embracing the essential habits that lead to greatness. Your story begins now.

Habit 1

Setting Clear Goals

Defining Your Path to Success

In the early morning light, as the world was just beginning to stir, Emily sat at her kitchen table with a steaming cup of coffee. It was a moment of rare tranquility in her hectic life. She knew she had a full day ahead, filled with responsibilities and obligations. But right now, in this serene solitude, she had a choice to make.

Emily had always harbored dreams of making a significant impact in her field. She had visions of leading her own team, launching groundbreaking projects, and leaving a lasting legacy. However, as the days turned into weeks and the weeks into years, those dreams had remained elusive, like distant stars in the night sky

Today, though, was different. As she took a sip of her coffee, she decided it was time to transform her aspirations into clear, actionable goals. She realized that having dreams was only the first step; to turn them into reality, she needed to define her path to success through setting clear goals.

The Power of Setting Clear Goals

Setting clear goals is the foundation upon which all great achievements are built. Without defined objectives, our dreams remain in the realm of wishful thinking, perpetually just out of reach. When Emily took that first step toward setting clear goals, she unwittingly ignited a powerful transformation within herself.

1.1 *Vision to Goals*

The journey from a vision to concrete goals is the bridge that many individuals never cross. In this section, we explore the process of transforming vague dreams into specific, measurable, and time-bound goals. You'll learn the art of visualizing your future and breaking it down into manageable steps.

1.2 *The SMART Approach*

Defining goals is not a haphazard process. It requires precision and structure. In Habit 1, we introduce you to the SMART approach, where goals are Specific, Measurable, Achievable, Relevant, and Time-bound. This technique will serve as your compass, guiding you toward successful goal setting.

1.3 *Overcoming Obstacles*

Every journey comes with its share of obstacles, and the path to success is no different. In this section, we address common challenges in setting and pursuing your goals. You'll discover strategies to overcome procrastination, self-doubt, and unexpected setbacks.

1.4 *The Power of Commitment*

An objective devoid of commitment is like a vessel without a leader. We'll delve into the importance of unwavering commitment to your goals and explore how it can propel you forward, even in the face of adversity.

1.5 *Case Study: Emily's Transformation*

Throughout this chapter, we'll follow Emily's inspiring journey as she sets clear goals and takes the necessary steps to redefine her path to success. Her story is a testament to the life-changing potential of this essential habit.

In the world of personal development, Habit 1 is the cornerstone that sets the stage for the subsequent habits to follow. As you embark on this chapter, you'll not only grasp the power of setting clear goals but also start your own journey toward a more successful and purpose-driven life. It's a path that, like Emily, you can walk with determination and hope, paving the way for a brighter, more fulfilling future.

Habit 2

Time Management and Prioritization

Making Every Moment Count

In the mosaic of our lives, time is the most precious and finite piece. It's a resource that cannot be replenished, paused, or rewound. Yet, it's also the canvas upon which we paint our achievements and shape our destiny. The manner in which we manage and prioritize our time is a profound reflection of our commitment to personal growth and success.

The art of time management and prioritization is not a mere collection of tips and tricks; it's a philosophy that can transform your life. It's about recognizing that every minute you spend is an investment in your future. To truly master Habit 2, "Time Management and Prioritization," is to grasp the essence of making every moment count.

The Value of Time

Every day, we are presented with a wealth of opportunities, challenges, and tasks. It's easy to become entangled in the web of urgencies, distractions, and unimportant demands. Habit 2 encourages us to take a step back and gain a deeper understanding of the value of time.

2.1 *The Time-Management Matrix*

Imagine a tool that could help you distinguish between what's truly important and what merely appears to be. The Time-Management Matrix, also known as the Eisenhower Matrix, does just that. It categorizes tasks into four quadrants based on urgency and importance, allowing you to prioritize with precision. By leveraging this tool, you become the architect of your schedule, ensuring that you allocate your time to those endeavors that lead to growth, success, and fulfillment.

2.2 *Prioritization Techniques*

The power of prioritization lies in your ability to identify which tasks deserve your immediate attention. Habit 2 introduces various prioritization techniques that empower you to make those decisions with confidence. Whether you opt for the ABCD method or the Pareto Principle, these techniques grant you clarity in a world often clouded by distractions.

2.3 *Overcoming Procrastination*

Procrastination is the silent thief of time and productivity. This habit offers strategies to combat this common nemesis. You'll learn to set realistic deadlines, break tasks into manageable steps, and silence the inner voice that tells you to delay. The triumph over procrastination is the gateway to reclaiming your moments and channeling them into your aspirations.

2.4 *Maximizing Efficiency*

Efficiency is about doing more with less. In this section, you'll explore how to optimize your work environment, streamline your daily routines, and delegate tasks when necessary. By doing so, you not only free up time for the meaningful but also find a rhythm of productivity that allows you to savor your moments rather than rush through them.

2.5 *Creating a Time Management System*

The culmination of Habit 2 is the creation of your personalized time management system. It is not a one-size-fits-all solution but a framework designed to harmonize with your unique goals and values. As you craft your schedule, you craft your life. It's an opportunity to seize each day with purpose and intention.

In the professional world, mastery of Habit 2 is a hallmark of success. It's the ability to command time, not in a rigid and stifling way, but in a manner that allows you to orchestrate your journey towards your objectives. To make every moment count is not just a matter of productivity; it's a philosophy that underscores your commitment to personal development and the pursuit of your dreams.

As you embrace Habit 2, you'll find that your days are not simply passing moments but purposeful strides toward your goals. It's a transformation that elevates your relationship with time from mere existence to an extraordinary journey. Join us on this path to unlock the potential of each minute and make every moment count in your quest for success and influence.

Habit 3

Effective Communication

Building Strong Relationships

In the tapestry of life, the relationships we form are the most precious threads, weaving the narrative of our journey. Effective communication is the art of crafting the connections that sustain us, inspire us, and propel us forward in both personal and professional spheres.

Effective communication isn't solely about transmitting information; it's the alchemy of understanding, trust, and empathy. It's the skill that transforms interactions into meaningful bonds and transforms ordinary moments into extraordinary memories.

The Essence of Building Strong Relationships

At the heart of effective communication lies the desire to nurture and fortify the bonds that enrich our lives. It's the recognition that the depth and quality of our relationships are intrinsically linked to our ability to communicate effectively.

3.1 *The Power of Authenticity*

Effective communication begins with being genuine, transparent, and true to oneself. Habit 3 teaches us that authenticity is the cornerstone of trust. By being authentic, we invite others to do the same, laying the foundation for strong and enduring connections.

3.2 *The Art of Empathetic Listening*

Listening with empathy is the gateway to understanding the thoughts, feelings, and needs of those we communicate with. In this habit, we delve into the art of empathetic listening, which goes beyond hearing words and extends into comprehending the emotions behind them.

3.3 Conflict Resolution and Constructive Feedback

In every relationship, there are moments of disagreement and discord. Habit 3 equips us with the tools to navigate these challenging waters. By providing constructive feedback and resolving conflicts with grace and respect, we strengthen our bonds rather than allowing them to fracture.

3.4 *Nonverbal Communication and Emotional Intelligence*

The unspoken language is a potent force in building strong relationships. This habit emphasizes the significance of nonverbal communication and emotional intelligence, enabling us to understand and respond to the emotions of those we connect with.

3.5 *Fostering Trust and Connection*

Trust is the currency of meaningful relationships. Habit 3 shows us how to cultivate trust through our words, actions, and consistency. Trust forms the bedrock upon which lasting connections are built.

Building strong relationships is not merely about surrounding yourself with people but about creating a network of support, inspiration, and mutual growth. It's about leaving a positive impact on those whose lives we touch and allowing them to do the same for us.

By mastering the art of effective communication and the principles of building strong relationships, you elevate your capacity to connect, inspire, and influence. It's the key to unlocking doors of opportunity, creating an environment of collaboration, and leaving a legacy of meaningful interactions.

Join us on this transformative journey to embrace the power of authentic communication, empathetic listening, and constructive resolution. In the realm of effective communication, you'll discover not only the tools for building strong relationships but also the path to a world of profound connections and lasting influence.

Habit 4

Self-Discipline and Willpower

Forging the Path to Personal Mastery

In the journey toward personal development and success, there is no greater ally than self-discipline and willpower. It is the linchpin that empowers individuals to stay resolute, overcome obstacles, and navigate the often tumultuous seas of life.

Self-discipline and willpower are the twin engines that drive us to set and achieve audacious goals, maintain consistency, and master our impulses. They are the forces that transform lofty ambitions into tangible achievements.

The Essence of Self-Discipline and Willpower

Habit 4 is about understanding that the true measure of character lies in our ability to control our actions, to persevere in the face of adversity, and to consistently make choices that align with our long-term aspirations.

4.1 *The Power of Self-Discipline*

Self-discipline is the practice of making deliberate choices that are in harmony with our goals and values. It's the ability to resist immediate temptations and distractions, even when they seem overwhelmingly enticing. Habit 4 delves into the principles of self-discipline and provides a roadmap for cultivating this essential trait.

4.2 *Willpower: The Engine of Change*

Willpower is the inner strength that propels us to initiate and maintain change. It's the force that fuels our determination to pursue what we believe is right, even in the face of discomfort or adversity. Habit 4 explores the science behind willpower and offers strategies for strengthening this vital attribute.

4.3 *Goal Setting and Motivation*

Self-discipline and willpower are closely linked to effective goal setting and motivation. In this section, you'll learn how to set clear, meaningful goals that serve as beacons to guide your actions. You'll also discover how to harness your internal motivation to sustain your journey.

4.4 *Overcoming Procrastination and Temptation*

Procrastination and temptations can be formidable obstacles on the path to self-discipline and willpower. This habit provides techniques for conquering procrastination and strategies for resisting the allure of immediate gratification.

4.5 *Building Resilience*

Resilience is the ability to bounce back from setbacks and failures. Habit 4 emphasizes the importance of resilience in developing self-discipline and willpower. You'll uncover how to view failures as opportunities for growth and use setbacks as stepping stones to success.

Self-discipline and willpower are not merely about resisting indulgence or exerting control; they are the cornerstones of personal mastery. They empower you to seize the reins of your life, sculpt your character, and fashion a future where your actions align with your highest aspirations.

By embracing the principles of self-discipline and willpower, you equip yourself with the tools to achieve any goal, overcome any challenge, and navigate the complex journey of personal development. It's the difference between merely setting intentions and translating them into remarkable achievements.

Habit 5

Continuous Learning

The Path to Lifelong Growth and Fulfillment

The most enduring thing one can have in the constantly changing fabric of life is dedication to continuous learning. This is the catalyst that propels individuals on a journey of lifelong growth and fulfillment.

This habit is more than the acquisition of knowledge; it is a mindset that seeks out opportunities for exploration, discovery, and self-improvement. It is the belief that the pursuit of wisdom and new skills is a lifelong endeavor.

The Essence of Continuous Learning

Habit 5 acknowledges that in a world of ceaseless change, those who embrace learning are the ones who adapt, thrive, and make an indelible impact.

5.1 *Cultivating a Growth Mindset*

A growth mindset is the belief that abilities and intelligence can be developed through effort and dedication. Habit 5 dives into the principles of cultivating this mindset, which is the foundation for continuous learning.

5.2 *Embracing Curiosity*

Curiosity is the spark that ignites the flames of learning. This habit encourages you to ask questions, explore new horizons, and challenge the status quo. Curiosity is the driving force behind discovering new insights and evolving your understanding of the world.

5.3 *Effective Learning Strategies*

Continuous learning is not just about acquiring knowledge; it's also about how you learn. Habit 5 explores effective learning strategies, including setting clear goals, leveraging the power of deliberate practice, and honing your critical thinking skills.

5.4 *The Role of Adaptability*

Adaptability is closely intertwined with continuous learning. In this section, you'll discover how learning equips you to adapt to changing circumstances, embrace innovation, and remain relevant in an ever-evolving world.

5.5 *A Commitment to Self-Improvement*

At its core, continuous learning is about a commitment to self-improvement. It's the acknowledgment that you are a work in progress, and there's always room for growth. You'll learn how to set learning goals and create a plan for continuous self-improvement.

Continuous learning is not a means to an end; it is the path itself. It is the recognition that the pursuit of knowledge and personal development is not bound by age, career stage, or circumstance. It is the key to remaining relevant, adaptable, and fulfilled in a world that is in constant flux.

By embracing the principles of continuous learning, you empower yourself to not only keep pace with change but to lead change. It's the difference between merely existing and thriving, between remaining stagnant and evolving into your best self.

Habit 6

Emotional Intelligence

The most common definition of emotional intelligence (EI) is the capacity to recognize, utilize, comprehend, regulate, and deal with emotions. Emotionally intelligent people are able to identify and categorize a wide range of emotions, distinguish between distinct emotions and assign the proper labels to each one, and modify their emotions in response to changing circumstances.

This habit is not about suppressing or controlling emotions but rather about understanding and harnessing their power for personal and interpersonal benefit. It is the skill of recognizing, managing, and empathizing with both your own emotions and those of others.

The Essence of Emotional Intelligence

Habit 6 is built on the premise that understanding and effectively managing emotions is pivotal to living a fulfilling and purpose-driven life.

6.1 *The Pillars of Emotional Intelligence*

Emotional intelligence consists of several key components, including self-awareness, self-regulation, motivation, empathy, and social skills. Emotional Intelligence delves into these pillars, providing a comprehensive understanding of each and offering strategies for their development.

6.2 *Self-Awareness: The Foundation*

Self-awareness is the cornerstone of emotional intelligence. It is the ability to recognize your own emotions, their impact on your thoughts and behavior, and their role in shaping your relationships. Emotional Intelligence guides you on the journey of self-discovery, helping you uncover your emotional triggers and patterns.

6.3 *Self-Regulation: Managing Your Emotions*

The skill of efficiently controlling your emotions is known as self-regulation. This section provides techniques for controlling impulsive reactions, handling stress, and making choices that align with your long-term goals.

6.4 *Empathy: Understanding Others*

The capacity to comprehend and experience another person's feelings is known as empathy. Emotional Intelligence emphasizes the importance of empathetic listening and perspective-taking. You'll learn how to connect on a deeper level with people by understanding their emotions and demonstrating genuine care.

6.5 *Building Positive Relationships*

Strong relationships are built on emotional intelligence. This habit explores the role of emotional intelligence in forging and nurturing healthy, positive connections with others. You'll discover how to communicate effectively, resolve conflicts, and build trust.

Emotional intelligence is not a soft skill but a potent force that shapes the quality of our personal and professional lives. It is the ability to make deliberate choices, respond thoughtfully to challenges, and create a supportive, empathetic environment for oneself and others.

By embracing the principles of emotional intelligence, you empower yourself to not only understand and regulate your own emotions but also to connect with others on a deeper level. It's the difference between merely coexisting with others and fostering relationships that thrive and enrich your life.

Habit 7

Adaptability and Resilience

Thriving in the Face of Change

In the previous chapters, we've journeyed through the landscapes of personal development, success, and influence. Now, as we stand on the precipice of Habit 7, the terrain shifts, and the metaphorical river of life begins to flow with greater intensity.

Habit 7 is the empowering crescendo that celebrates adaptability and resilience. It's this habit that invites you to embrace change not as an adversary but as a conductor of growth and transformation.

This habit is more than a mere tool for survival; it's a mindset that propels you forward, even when the path is uncertain, the ground shaky, and the challenges daunting. Habit 7 encourages you to be not just a passive observer of change but an active participant in shaping your destiny.

The Essence of Adaptability and Resilience

Habit 7 is rooted in the understanding that change is the only constant in life. It's about equipping yourself with the tools to not just endure change but to flourish within it.

7.1 *Embracing Changer*

Change is the pulse of existence, and Habit 7 guides you to not only accept change but to welcome it. You'll learn how to view change as an opportunity for growth and transformation, rather than as a disruption.

7.2 *Navigating Uncertainty*

Uncertainty is an inherent part of life, and this habit provides strategies for navigating the unpredictable waters of uncertainty. It teaches you how to maintain your composure, focus, and determination during tumultuous times.

7.3 *Developing Resilience*

Bouncing back from adversity is the art of resilience. Habit 7 underscores the significance of resilience and equips you with techniques to strengthen your emotional fortitude, manage stress, and see challenges as stepping stones to success.

7.4 *Problem-Solving and Innovation*

Adaptability is essential for thriving, not simply for survival; it's about thriving. This section explores how adaptability can foster creativity, innovation, and a problem-solving mindset. You'll discover how to use change as a catalyst for personal and professional growth.

7.5 *Thriving in Transition*

Adaptability and resilience are not mere skills; they are the keys to embracing the journey, to not merely endure change but to harness it as a powerful force for your advancement.

Habit 7 is your invitation to not just survive the storms but to navigate them skillfully and emerge stronger on the other side. It's the difference between being a passive recipient of change and being an active conductor of your life's orchestration.

Habit 8

Networking and Building Connections

Leveraging Your Relationships

Habit 8, "Networking and Building Connections," stands as a beacon illuminating the significance of relationships, connections, and the power of your network.

This habit goes beyond the mere act of meeting people; it's about strategically leveraging your relationships to create opportunities, foster collaboration, and amplify your influence. It's the skill of not only forming connections but nurturing and utilizing them to achieve your goals.

The Essence of Networking and Building Connections

Habit 8 acknowledges that in today's interconnected world, your success is profoundly influenced by the people you know and the relationships you cultivate.

8.1 *The Power of Your Network*

Your network is your greatest asset. This habit delves into the importance of maintaining and expanding your network, highlighting how it can open doors, provide support, and offer invaluable insights.

8.2 *Strategic Relationship Building*

Effective networking is not a matter of chance but a strategy. Habit 8 offers techniques for building and maintaining relationships with purpose, from setting clear networking goals to nurturing mutually beneficial connections.

8.3 *Collaboration and Resource Sharing*

Your network is a treasure trove of resources, talents, and opportunities. This section explores the art of collaboration, resource sharing, and how to maximize the potential of your network.

8.4 *Influence and Impact*

Habit 8 also delves into the ability to influence and inspire others within your network. It's about being a valuable contributor, fostering trust, and leaving a positive impact.

8.5 *Ethical and Authentic Networking*

Authenticity and ethics are core to effective networking. This habit emphasizes the importance of integrity, transparency, and building connections based on trust and shared values.

Networking and building connections is not about superficial interactions but about the deliberate and strategic cultivation of relationships that serve your personal and professional growth. It's the difference between collecting business cards and creating a network of allies, mentors, and collaborators who can help you reach new heights.

In this transformative journey toward mastering the art of networking and building connections. In the realm of networking and building connections, you'll not only unlock the secrets to leveraging your relationships but also pave the way to a life filled with opportunities, collaboration, and an expansive network that can propel you toward your aspirations.

Habit 9

Problem-Solving and Critical thinking

Making informed Decisions

Problem solving and critical thinking is referred to as the ability to apply information, facts, and data to solve issues successfully. This doesn't imply that you have to know the answer right away; rather, it just calls for quick thinking, problem-solving, and assessment skills. One of the deep learning skills that has been found to be crucial to people's growth is critical thinking and problem solving.

This habit is the key to sharpening your ability to analyze, assess, and solve challenges and make decisions rooted in wisdom and discernment. It's not merely about addressing problems; it's about transforming them into opportunities for growth. Habit 9 empowers you to approach issues with clarity, evaluate options systematically, and ultimately make well-informed decisions that align with your goals and values.

The Essence of Problem-Solving and Critical Thinking

Habit 9 acknowledges that the ability to navigate complex issues and make sound decisions is a cornerstone of success and personal development.

9.1 *The Art of Critical Thinking*

The basis for efficient problem-solving and decision-making is critical thinking. This habit delves into the principles of critical thinking, including analyzing information, evaluating evidence, and drawing reasoned conclusions.

9.2 *Problem-Solving Strategies*

This habit provides a toolbox of problem-solving strategies, from defining the problem and generating solutions to implementing decisions and evaluating outcomes. You'll learn how to tackle challenges with a structured approach.

9.3 *Decision-Making Frameworks*

Effective decisions are not made in a vacuum; they are guided by decision-making frameworks. Habit 9 explores various decision-making models, such as cost-benefit analysis, risk assessment, and ethical considerations, to help you make choices that are well-informed and aligned with your values.

9.4 *Critical Analysis*

Critical analysis is the art of examining information, arguments, and situations with depth and precision. This habit equips you with the skills to critically assess data, perspectives, and potential solutions, ensuring that your decisions are based on a solid foundation.

9.5 *Ethical Decision-Making*

Ethics play a crucial role in decision-making. This habit emphasizes the importance of making decisions that are not only logical and practical but also ethical and aligned with your principles.

Habit 9 is your pathway to not only addressing challenges but turning them into stepping stones for growth. It's the difference between reacting to problems impulsively and proactively solving them with wisdom and a structured approach.

In the realm of Habit 9, you'll not only unlock the secrets to making informed decisions but also pave the way to a life filled with thoughtful analysis, effective solutions, and choices that lead you closer to your desired future.

Habit 10

Creativity and Innovation

Thinking Outside the Box

"Creativity and Innovation," emerges as the vibrant, dynamic thread that celebrates the art of thinking beyond boundaries, igniting ideas, and fostering innovation.

This habit isn't just about brainstorming; it's the ability to stretch your imagination, challenge the status quo, and transcend conventional thinking. Habit 10 empowers you to infuse creativity into your problem-solving, decision-making, and the pursuit of new horizons.

The Essence of Creativity and Innovation

Habit 10 recognizes that creativity and innovation are not luxuries but vital forces that drive progress and success in the modern world.

10.1 *Cultivating Creative Thinking*

Creative thinking is the foundation of innovation. This habit delves into the principles of nurturing your creative spirit, including embracing curiosity, embracing ambiguity, and fostering a growth mindset.

10.2 *Idea Generation and Exploration*

Generating and exploring ideas is a core component of creativity. Habit 10 provides techniques for ideation, brainstorming, and the exploration of uncharted territories of thought.

10.3 *Breaking Down Barriers*

Innovation often involves overcoming mental barriers. This section explores how to challenge assumptions, confront biases, and embrace unconventional solutions.

10.4 *Implementing Innovative Solutions*

It's not enough to generate ideas; innovation also requires effective implementation. Habit 10 provides strategies for bringing creative solutions to life, including project management, prototyping, and feedback loops.

10.5 *Embracing a Culture of Innovation*

Innovation thrives within a culture that encourages it. This habit emphasizes the importance of fostering an environment where creativity is not only encouraged but celebrated.

Creativity and Innovation is your pathway to not just thinking beyond the box but redefining the box itself. It's the difference between adhering to the status quo and pushing the boundaries of what's possible, between solving problems conventionally and uncovering transformative, groundbreaking solutions.

Habit 11

Health and Wellness

Nurturing Your Body and Mind

Health and Wellness is not confined to mere physical fitness; it encompasses the art of cultivating a symbiotic relationship between your physical and mental well-being. It empowers you to adopt a lifestyle that prioritizes health, vitality, and a harmonious equilibrium of the body and mind.

The Essence of Health and Wellness

Health and Wellness recognizes that true success and fulfillment can only be attained when your physical and mental faculties are in harmony. It's about understanding that optimal health is the cornerstone of a meaningful life.

11.1 *Physical Health and Fitness*

Physical health forms the bedrock of overall well-being. This habit explores the principles of maintaining a healthy body, incorporating regular exercise, nourishing nutrition, and sufficient rest into your daily routine.

11.2 *Mental Health and Resilience*

Mental health is the underpinning of emotional balance and resilience. It delves into the importance of mindfulness, stress management, and strategies for nurturing a robust mental well-being.

11.3 *Holistic Wellness*

Holistic wellness is the amalgamation of various facets of your life, including physical, mental, emotional, and even spiritual. Habit 11 emphasizes the significance of approaching health and wellness as an integrated whole, taking into account all these dimensions.

11.4 *Stress Management and Work-Life Balance*

Balancing the demands of life and managing stress is critical. This habit provides insights into creating a balanced lifestyle that nurtures your body and mind, from managing work-life equilibrium to embracing relaxation and leisure activities.

11.5 *Preventive Health Measures*

Preventive health measures play a pivotal role in maintaining well-being. This section covers the significance of regular health check-ups, early disease detection, and taking proactive steps to safeguard your health.

Habit 11 is your pathway to not just living but thriving. It's the difference between mere existence and a life imbued with vitality, resilience, and the capacity to savor each day to the fullest. By embracing this habit, you lay the foundation for a future that is not just successful but profoundly fulfilling.

Habit 12

Financial Management

Securing Your Financial Future

Financial management entails planning, organizing, directing, and controlling the enterprise's financial activities such as purchase and utilization of funds. It comprises applying broad management concepts to the financial resources of the business.

Financial Management unfolds as a vital thread dedicated to the strategic and prudent handling of your finances.

Management of finances transcends mere monetary matters; it encompasses the art of securing your financial future through smart financial planning, budgeting, investing, and wealth-building strategies. It also empowers you to attain financial stability and the peace of mind that comes with it.

The Essence of Financial Management

Habit 12 underscores that financial well-being is an integral aspect of a successful and fulfilled life. It's about recognizing that taking control of your finances is not just about money; it's about securing your future.

12.1 *Budgeting and Financial Planning*

Sound financial management commences with effective budgeting and planning. This habit explores the principles of creating a financial plan, budgeting wisely, and setting achievable financial goals.

12.2 *Saving and Investing*

Financial security is founded on saving and investing wisely. Habit 12 delves into the art of saving, investment strategies, and understanding the principles of risk and return.

12.3 *Debt Management*

Effective financial management also involves prudent debt management. This section provides insights into managing debt, reducing interest costs, and devising a strategy for debt elimination.

12.4 *Financial Literacy*

Financial literacy is the cornerstone of effective financial management. This habit emphasizes the significance of understanding financial terms, investment options, and staying informed about economic trends.

Financial Management is your pathway to not just monetary security but financial peace of mind. It's the difference between financial stress and the freedom to pursue your dreams, between living paycheck to paycheck and securing your future with confidence.

Habit 13

Giving Back and Philanthropy

The Power of Contribution

Giving Back and Philanthropy is a shining theme that highlights the significant influence of making a positive impact on the world.

This habit goes beyond personal gain; it's the art of recognizing the significance of giving, sharing, and contributing to the well-being of others and the greater community. Habit 13 empowers you to harness the transformative power of philanthropy and make a positive impact on the world.

The Essence of Giving Back and Philanthropy

Giving Back and Philanthropy recognizes that personal growth is intrinsically linked to contributing to the welfare of others. It's about understanding that making a difference in the lives of others not only benefits them but also enriches your own life.

13.1 *The Joy of Giving*

Giving is a source of profound joy. This habit explores the joy that comes from contributing to charitable causes, volunteering, and being of service to others.

13.2 *Philanthropic Endeavors*

Philanthropy is not just about giving money; it's about supporting causes and organizations that align with your values. Habit 13 delves into the art of philanthropic endeavors and the various ways you can make a positive impact.

13.3 *Volunteering and Community Engagement*

Getting involved in your community and actively volunteering is a crucial component of giving back. This section provides insights into the importance of community engagement and how you can contribute your time and skills.

13.4 *Social Responsibility*

Social responsibility is an integral part of philanthropy. This habit emphasizes the significance of supporting initiatives that address social and environmental issues, making the world a better place for current and future generations.

13.5 *The Ripple Effect of Contribution*

Your contribution doesn't just impact individuals; it has a ripple effect on the world. Habit 13 highlights how giving back not only makes a difference in the lives of others but also contributes to a more compassionate and just society.

Not only will philanthropy and giving back help you grow personally, but they will also leave a legacy of positive change. It's the distinction between leading a life that serves solely one's personal interests and one that transforms the earth and opens doors for a better future for all.

Habit 14

Leadership and Influence

Inspiring Others

The ability to persuade is one definition of leadership. Instead of using force, an effective leader encourages followers to take action by appealing to their desire and conviction in the vision and goals that the leader has stated.

The ability to wield influence is an essential leadership skill. To affect someone's attitudes, decisions, actions, and opinions is to exert influence over them. Influence should not be mistaken for authority or control. It's not about lying to get what you desire. It entails figuring out what motivates people to be dedicated and using that knowledge to increase productivity and produce desirable results.

This habit is not confined to leadership roles alone; it encompasses the capacity to influence and inspire, whether you lead a team, an organization, or your own life. It also empowers you to cultivate the qualities of an effective leader and influencer, inspiring positive change in those around you.

The Essence of Leadership and Influence

Leader recognizes that the ability to lead and influence is a fundamental aspect of personal and professional growth. It's about understanding that leadership is not about authority but about inspiring others to achieve their best potential.

14.1 *Leading by Example*

Effective leadership begins with setting a positive example. This habit explores the importance of leading by demonstrating integrity, commitment, and a strong work ethic.

14.2 *Inspiring Vision and Purpose*

Leadership involves creating a compelling vision and purpose that motivates and guides others.

Habit 14 delves into the art of inspiring vision, setting clear goals, and instilling a sense of purpose within your team or community.

14.3 *Effective Communication*

Communication is a cornerstone of leadership and influence. This section provides insights into the importance of clear and empathetic communication, active listening, and the power of effective persuasion.

14.4 *Building and Empowering Teams*

Leadership extends to building and empowering teams. Habit 14 emphasizes the significance of creating a cohesive team, delegating responsibilities, and empowering team members to reach their full potential.

14.5 *Positive Impact and Legacy*

Leadership is not just about the present but also the legacy you leave behind. This habit highlights the importance of making a positive impact on the lives of others and the broader community, leaving a lasting legacy.

Your path to success and development, not only for yourself but also for those you lead and influence, is through leadership and influence. It's the distinction between leading by example and motivating others, between accomplishing your objectives and enabling others to fulfill theirs.

Habit 15

Review and Reflection

Tracking Your Progress

Review and reflection shines as a beacon, illuminating the significance of assessing your journey, learning from experiences, and constantly improving.

This habit is not just about the actions you take; it's the art of periodically pausing, looking back, and evaluating your progress. Habit 15 empowers you to embrace a reflective mindset, providing insights into the successes and challenges that have shaped your personal development.

The Essence of Review and Reflection

The habit of review and reflection acknowledges that personal growth is an ongoing, dynamic process that requires self-awareness and the willingness to learn and adapt. It's about understanding that continuous improvement comes from reviewing your path and reflecting on your actions.

15.1 *Setting Milestones and Goals*

Review and reflection begin with setting clear milestones and goals. This habit explores the importance of defining your objectives and regularly evaluating your progress toward them.

15.2 *Analyzing Achievements and Setbacks*

Achievements and setbacks are part of any journey. Habit 15 delves into the art of analyzing your accomplishments and challenges, drawing lessons from both, and using them to refine your path forward.

15.3 *Self-Assessment and Growth*

Self-assessment is the cornerstone of personal development. This section provides insights into self-reflection, self-awareness, and the power of acknowledging your strengths and areas for improvement.

15.4 *Adaptation and Planning*

Review and reflection are not just about looking back; they're about looking forward. Habit 15 emphasizes the significance of adapting your strategies, refining your plans, and continuously learning and growing.

15.5 *Celebrating Success and Cultivating Resilience*

Success is worth celebrating, and resilience is cultivated through reflection. This habit highlights the importance of acknowledging your achievements and building the resilience to face future challenges.

Conclusion

Embracing a Lifetime of Personal Development

As we draw the final curtain on this transformative journey through the 15 essential habits for personal development, we stand at the crossroads of the past, present, and future. It is here, in the realm of culmination, that we find the essence of personal development.

Throughout this exploration, we have delved into the art of self-improvement, uncovering the vital habits that can propel us towards our aspirations and full potential. We have witnessed the significance of setting clear goals, managing time, mastering communication, adapting to change, and nurturing our physical and mental well-being, among many other valuable facets of personal growth.

Yet, personal development is not a one-time event but a lifelong commitment, an ever-unfolding journey. It is in the continued practice of these habits that we find the true power of transformation. In the daily application of these principles, we cultivate resilience, clarity, and the unwavering drive to become the best version of ourselves.

In concluding our exploration, we understand that personal development is not about reaching a finite destination but embracing a lifetime of growth, self-discovery, and the relentless pursuit of excellence. It is about understanding that each day presents a new opportunity to apply these habits, learn from our experiences, and evolve.

So, as we step away from these pages and into the ever-flowing river of life, let us carry with us the wisdom of Habit 15, the art of review and reflection. Let us track our progress, acknowledge our achievements, and learn from our setbacks. Let us adapt, plan, celebrate, and cultivate resilience in the face of challenges.

Embracing a lifetime of personal development is not a journey marked by a single finish line but a continuum of self-discovery, growth, and the unwavering pursuit of excellence. It is a journey that molds us into the architects of our destinies, the shapers of our dreams, and the beacons of inspiration to those around us.

In the end, our personal development is not measured by the destination but by the steps we take, the habits we nurture, and the lives we touch along the way. As we continue this lifelong journey, let us remember that our potential is boundless, our aspirations are limitless, and our capacity for growth is infinite. The adventure is still ongoing, and the best is yet to come.

www.ingramcontent.com/pod-product-compliance
Lightning Source LLC
Chambersburg PA
CBHW071059260726
48661CB00006B/2341